David and Goliath

Originally published by Hunt and Thorpe 1993
Reissued in 1997
ISBN 1-85608-324-1
Reprinted 2001

The CIP catalogue record for this book is available from the British Library.

Printed in Malaysia

David and Goliath

Rhona Pipe

Illustrated by
Stephen Walsh

John Hunt
Publishing Limited

When David was a boy
his job was to look after the sheep.
There were lions and bears
in the hills,
but David was a good shot
with his catapult,
and God helped him
to keep the sheep safe.

When David was a boy
his country was at war.
Once, the enemy army was only
about twenty miles away
from David's farm.
David's three big brothers went off
to fight for King Saul.

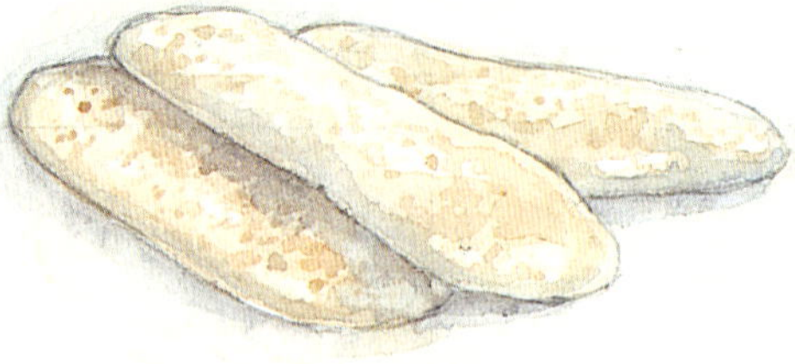

After a while
David's dad said,
'Take this bread and cheese
to your brothers,
and see how they are getting on
in the army.'

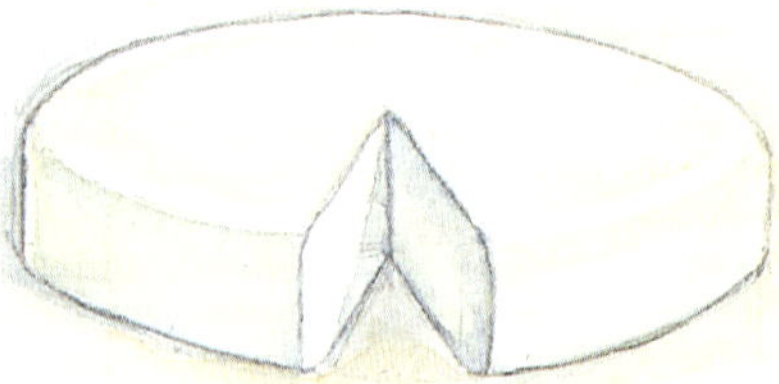

A man came out from the enemy lines.
He was a giant of a man,
close on three metres tall.
He yelled out:
'Pick a man to fight me.
Go on! I dare you!
Whoever wins, wins the war!'

'Oh — er — help!'
said King Saul's men.
'We're done for!'

But David said,
'He's in for a nasty shock.
God is on our side.
What's the reward
for killing that man who
doesn't love God?'

David's brother said,
'You cheeky brat!
What are you doing here?
Run off back home to your sheep.'

'I was only asking!' David said,
and went to find King Saul.

‘I’ll fight the giant Goliath for you,’
David said.
‘And I’ll kill him.’

‘How can you?’ asked Saul.
‘You’re only a kid.’

‘To God, Goliath is nothing,’
said David.
‘God saved me from lions and bears.
He’ll save me from Goliath.’

'All right,' said Saul.
'You have a go,
and God go with you.'
Saul gave David his
armour and sword,
but they were far too big.

So David went out with
his shepherd's stick and his catapult
and his trust in God.

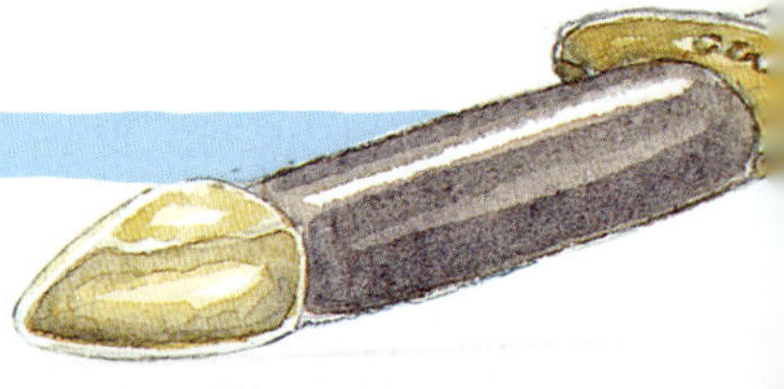

'Ha! Ha!' said Goliath.
'What's that stick for? A dog?
Ha! Ha!
Come on,
I'll make mincemeat out of you,
baby face!'

David put a stone in his catapult.

Round and round went the catapult.
Then zing! Out flew the stone —
and — crash!
Down fell Goliath.
David had won.

'Now the whole world knows
that God saves the people
who trust him,' David said.